I Can Listen to English! 2

KB197290

 Happy House

Dear Teachers and Parents,

Welcome to Happy House **"I Can Listen to English!"**

Happy House Listening is designed to meet the needs and interests of children. It aims to help children develop and improve the listening skills necessary to communicate in a fun environment. The full-color illustrations are based on a creative storyline that includes funny characters like Toby and Cory, elves who live in the attic. The fantastic story encourages children to build their English listening skills. Happy House Listening is a three-level course containing 10 units, and after every five units, four-page reviews for each level. Each unit features a question and an answer with 8~10 alternative words. A topic which draws on the everyday lives and experiences of children with a fun story has been added. This book is child-centered in order to benefit young children and to prepare them for the fruitful use of English listening at a higher level.

● E2K Contents

A creative group that provides quality contents and educational services in English for ESL and EFL students.
The goal of E2K is to make the finest quality materials to make learning English more enjoyable for students.

TABLE OF CONTENTS

HOW TO USE
"I CAN LISTEN TO ENGLISH!"

Chant Listening

It helps to present new structures and new words in a fun and easy way. And it also provides motivation for listening.

Sentence Listening

This listening exercise reinforces the previous pages to help students learn sentence structures.

Word Listening

This listening exercise provides thorough practice in using new words.

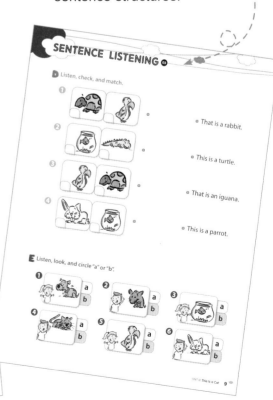

Speak & Play

This oral activity encourages communication by playing a game.

Writing

These listening activities give learners the opportunity to practice structures and words by writing.

Phonics Listening

This phonics story gives learners the chance to read short stories. This listening and writing activity contains questions designed to improve students' understanding of phonics rules.

Review

These are systematic recycling and review pages.

Phonics Review

The various questions in this section help learners to understand phonics rules and improve their listening, reading, and writing skills. They also help increase learners' vocabularies.

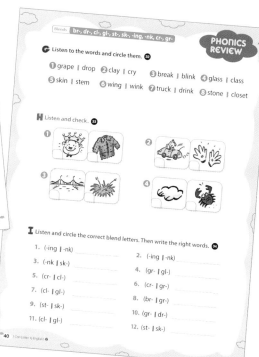

UNIT 01

This Is a Cat

CHANT LISTENING 01

A Listen and chant.
Then circle the pets you hear in the chant.

B Listen, write the number, and match.

goldfish   parrot   turtle   dog

C Listen, look, and circle.

1    goldfish   (iguana)   turtle

2    cat   dog   rabbit

3    iguana   cat   hamster

4    turtle   goldfish   rabbit

D Listen, check, and match.

1.   That is a rabbit.

2.   This is a turtle.

3.   That is an iguana.

4.   This is a parrot.

E Listen, look, and circle "a" or "b".

1.  a b

2.  a b

3.  a b

4.  a b

5.  a b

6.  a b

SPEAK & PLAY

F Ask and answer with your partner. Follow the steps below.

What is this/that?

This is a/an _____.
That is a/an _____.

dog   cat   parrot
goldfish   turtle   rabbit
iguana   hamster

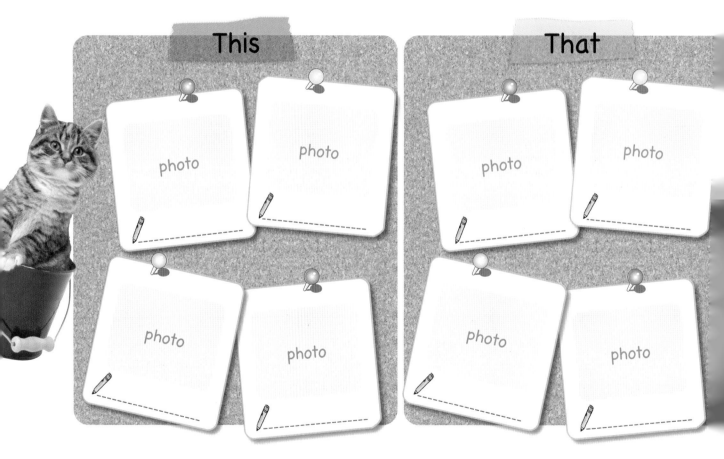

Step 1. Find a partner.

Step 2. Your partner asks you a question, and then you answer it.

Step 3. Find the Pet Sticker for your answer.

Step 4. Attach the sticker to the board, and then write the word in the blank.

WRITING

Listen, circle, and write. 04

| goldfish | iguana | rabbit | turtle |

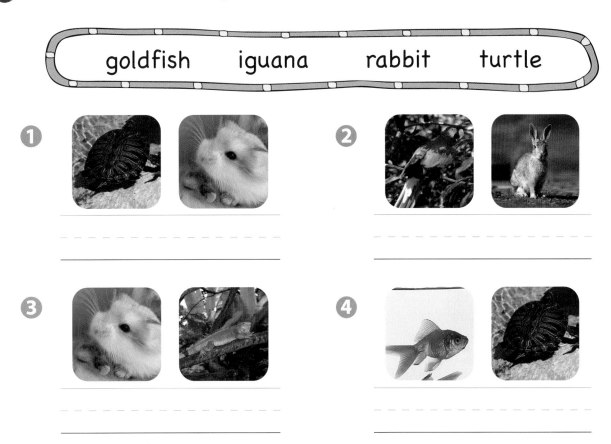

① _____

② _____

③ _____

④ _____

H Read, look, and complete the sentences using "a" or "an".

① **Q** What is this?

A This is _____ .

iguana

② **Q** What is that?

A That is _____ .

parrot

PHONICS LISTENING 05

I Listen and read the phonics story.

What is this?
This is my breakfast.
A drink and bread.
Bring me a drink.

What is that?
That is my dresser.
A dryer and a brush.
Please dry my hair.

J Listen and write the correct blend letters and a word.

drink   bread   bring   dresser   brush   dryer

1. _____ ➕ ead ➖ _____

2. _____ ➕ ing ➖ _____

3. _____ ➕ esser ➖ _____

4. _____ ➕ ink ➖ _____

5. _____ ➕ yer ➖ _____

6. _____ ➕ ush ➖ _____

UNIT 02

It's Eleven o'clock

A Listen and chant.
Then circle the times you hear in the chant.

WORD LISTENING 07

B Listen, circle, and match.

1 ○   ○ eleven o'clock

2 ○   ○ twelve o'clock

3 ○   ○ twelve fifteen

4 ○   ○ eleven fifty

C Listen, check, and circle the word.

1 eleven twenty | eleven ten

2 eleven forty | eleven thirty

3 eleven forty | twelve ten

4 twelve o'clock | twelve ten

D Listen, check, and match.

①   ○   ○ It's eleven ten.

②   ○   ○ It's eleven thirty.

③   ○   ○ It's eleven fifty.

④   ○   ○ It's twelve fifteen.

E Listen, look, and circle "a" or "b".

①  a   b

②  a   b

③  a   b

④  a   b

⑤  a   b

⑥  a   b

SPEAK & PLAY

F Ask and answer with your partner. Follow the steps below.

What time is it?

It's _____.

eleven o'clock   twelve o'clock
twelve fifteen   eleven fifty
eleven twenty   twelve thirty
twelve ten   eleven forty

Step 1. Find a partner.

Step 2. Your partner asks you a question, and then you answer it.

Step 3. Find the Word Sticker for your answer.

Step 4. Draw your time in the clock, and then attach the sticker below the clock.

WRITING

 Listen, circle, and write. **09**

> twelve fifteen   eleven o'clock   eleven twenty   eleven thirty

1

_____

2

_____

3

_____

4

_____

H Read, look, and complete the sentences.

1 Q What time is it?

A It's _____ .

eleven fifty

2 Q What time is it?

A It's _____ .

twelve o'clock

I Listen and read the phonics story.

Give me some clay.
Give me some glue.
Draw two gloves.
Gloves on the hands.
Write 12 numbers.

Here is a clock!
A clock in the class.
What time is it?
It's 9 o'clock.

J Listen and circle the correct blend letters. Then write the right words.

glove   clay   clock   glue   class   glass

1. (cl- | gl-) _____

2. (cl- | gl-) _____

3. (cl- | gl-) _____

4. (cl- | gl-) _____

5. (cl- | gl-) _____

6. (cl- | gl-) _____

UNIT 03

There Are Three Bedrooms

CHANT LISTENING ⑪

A Listen and chant.
Then circle the rooms of the house you hear in the chant.

B Listen, write the number, and match.

○   ○   ○   ○

○   ○   ○   ○

(living room)   (kitchen)   (garage)   (bedroom)

C Listen, look, and circle.

①

bedroom   bathroom   dining room

②

room   dining room   attic

③

attic   bathroom   kitchen

④

garage   bedroom   basement

SENTENCE LISTENING 🔞

D Listen, check, and match.

1 ○   ○ There is one living room.

2 ○   ○ There are two bathrooms.

3 ○   ○ There is one garage.

4 ○   ○ There are four bedrooms.

E Listen, look, and circle "a" or "b".

1  a / b

2  a / b

3  a / b

4  a / b

5  a / b

6  a / b

SPEAK & PLAY

F Ask and answer with your partner. Follow the steps below.

How many _____ is/are there?

There is/are _____.

one living room	two bathrooms
three bedrooms	two dining rooms
one attic	two kitchens
one basement	one garage

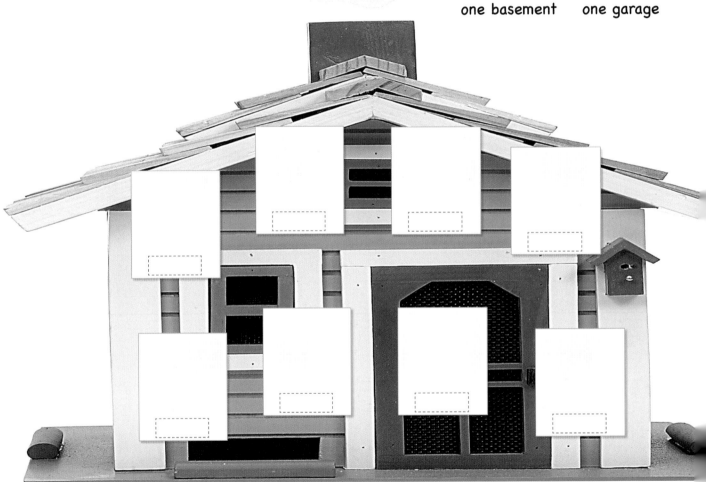

Step 1. 🖐 Find a partner.

Step 2. 🖐 Your partner asks you a question, and then you answer it.

Step 3. 🖐 Find the Room and Word Sticker for your answer.

Step 4. 🖐 Attach the sticker to the house.

WRITING

bathroom   dining room   kitchen   living room

1

_____

_____

2

_____

_____

3

_____

_____

4

_____

_____

H Read, look, and complete the sentences.

1 Q How many _____ are there?

A There is _____.

one attic

2 Q How many _____ are there?

A There are _____.

two bedrooms

I Listen and read the phonics story.

Skunk buys steak.
Skirt with stars.
Skates are sky blue.
Storybooks on the steps.

How many stores are there?
There are four stores.

Grocery store. Clothes store.
Sports store. Bookstore.

J Listen and write the correct blend letters and a word.

skunk	skate	skirt	star	steak	step

1. _____ ✚ irt ⊖ _____

2. _____ ✚ ar ⊖ _____

3. _____ ✚ ate ⊖ _____

4. _____ ✚ unk ⊖ _____

5. _____ ✚ eak ⊖ _____

6. _____ ✚ ep ⊖ _____

UNIT 04

I'm Going to the Park

CHANT LISTENING 16

A Listen and chant.
Then circle the places you hear in the chant.

B Listen, circle, and match.

①    ○   ○ library

②   ○   ○ post office

③   ○   ○ museum

④    ○   ○ department store

C Listen, check, and circle the word.

①

bank ┃ airport

②

library ┃ hospital

③

park ┃ museum

④

bank ┃ department store

SENTENCE LISTENING ⑱

D Listen, check, and match.

①
- I'm going to the hospital.

②
- I'm going to the post office.

③
- I'm going to the library.

④
- I'm going to the department store.

E Listen, look, and circle "a" or "b".

①  a / b

②  a / b

③  a / b

④  a / b

⑤  a / b

⑥  a / b

SPEAK & PLAY

F Ask and answer with your partner. Follow the steps below.

Where are you going?

I'm going to the _____.

museum   library   post office
department store   airport
hospital   park   bank

Step 1. Find a partner.

Step 2. Your partner asks you a question, and then you answer it.

Step 3. Find the Place Sticker for your answer.

Step 4. Attach the sticker below the word.

WRITING

 Listen, circle, and write. 🔟9

airport	department store	library	museum

❶

_____

_____

❷

_____

_____

❸

_____

_____

❹

_____

_____

H Read, look, and complete the sentences using "the".

❶ **Q** Where are you going?

A I'm going to _____ .

bank

❷ **Q** Where are you going?

A I'm going to _____ .

park

I Listen and read the phonics story.

I have a pink ring.
I have pink ink.
I want a pink sink.

Bring some paint.
Paint in the trunk.

Where are you going?
I'm going to open the trunk.

J Listen and circle the correct blend letters. Then write the right words.

ink   bring   trunk   sink   ring   pink

1. (-ing | -nk) _____

2. (-ing | -nk) _____

3. (-ing | -nk) _____

4. (-ing | -nk) _____

5. (-ing | -nk) _____

6. (-ing | -nk) _____

UNIT 05

It's on the Bed

CHANT LISTENING 🄬

A Listen and chant.
Then circle the room objects you hear in the chant.

B Listen, write the number, and match.

chair   desk   bookshelf   drawer

C Listen, look, and circle.

1    closet   bookshelf   desk

2    chair   bed   lamp

3    bed   desk   drawer

4 chair   curtain   closet

SENTENCE LISTENING ㉓

D Listen, check, and match.

1. ○ It's under the desk.

2. ○ It's by the chair.

3. ○ It's on the bookshelf.

4. ○ It's in the closet.

E Listen, look, and circle "a" or "b".

1  a / b

2  a / b

3  a / b

4  a / b

5  a / b

6  a / b

F Ask and answer with your partner. Follow the steps below.

Where is it?

It's on/in/by/under the _____.

drawer	chair	desk
bookshelf	closet	lamp
bed	curtain	

Step 1. Find a partner.

Step 2. Your partner asks you a question, and then you answer it.

Step 3. Find the Ball Sticker for your answer.

Step 4. Attach the Ball Sticker to the right place.

WRITING

G Listen, circle, and write. 24

bookshelf   closet   curtain   drawer

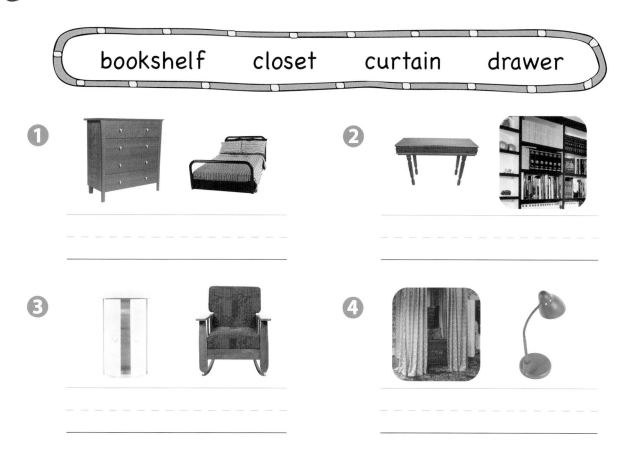

❶ _____

❷ _____

❸ _____

❹ _____

H Read, look, and complete the sentences using "on/in/by/under" and "the".

❶ Q Where is it?

A It's _____ .

bed

❷ Q Where is it?

A It's _____ .

desk

r-Blends **cr-, gr-**

I Listen and read the phonics story.

Happy Birthday, Greg!

Greg wears a crown.
He eats grapes.
Greg crawls.
He sees a cricket.
The cricket jumps.

Where is the cricket?
It's under the desk.

J Listen and write the correct blend letters and a word.

| crab   crown   cricket   crawl   green   cry |

1. _____ ⊕ een ⊖ _____   2. _____ ⊕ ab ⊖ _____

3. _____ ⊕ y ⊖ _____   4. _____ ⊕ own ⊖ _____

5. _____ ⊕ icket ⊖ _____   6. _____ ⊕ awl ⊖ _____

REVIEW 1 Units 1~5

A Listen and write the letter "a", "b", or "c". 26

1

2

3

4

B Listen, unscramble the words, and match. 27

1 eeelvn ➔ e_____ ○   ○

2 alibyrr ➔ l_____ ○   ○

3 werdra ➔ d_____ ○   ○

4 rgagea ➔ g_____ ○   ○

Listen and match. 🔢28

1 (What time is it?) ▫   ▫ (This is a cat.)

2 (Where is it?) ▫   ▫ (There are four bedrooms.)

3 (What is this?) ▫   ▫ (It's under the chair.)

4 (Where are you going?) ▫   ▫ (I'm going to the museum.)

5 (How many bedrooms are there?) ▫   ▫ (It's eleven o'clock.)

D Listen, find the picture, and write the number. 🔢29

 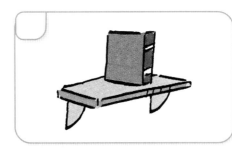

E Listen, write the number, and match. 🔵30

☐ Where is he? ◦	◦ There are two dogs.
☐ Where is she going? ◦	◦ That is a desk.
☐ What is that? ◦	◦ He's in the bathroom.
☐ How many dogs are there? ◦	◦ She's going to the bank.

F Listen, look, and complete the sentences. 🔵31

attic   chairs   o'clock   four   in   eleven

❶

Q How many chairs are there?

A There are _____ _____.

❷

Q Where is she?

A She is _____ the _____.

❸

Q What time is it?

A It's _____ _____.

PHONICS REVIEW

G Listen to the words and circle them. **32**

1 grape | drop 2 clay | cry 3 break | blink 4 glass | class

5 skin | stem 6 wing | wink 7 truck | drink 8 stone | closet

H Listen and check. **33**

1    2

3    4

I Listen and circle the correct blend letters. Then write the right words. **34**

1. (-ing | -nk) _____   2. (-ing | -nk) _____

3. (-nk | sk-) _____   4. (gr- | gl-) _____

5. (cr- | cl-) _____   6. (cr- | gr-) _____

7. (cl- | gl-) _____   8. (br- | gr-) _____

9. (st- | sk-) _____   10. (gr- | dr-) _____

11. (cl- | gl-) _____   12. (st- | sk-) _____

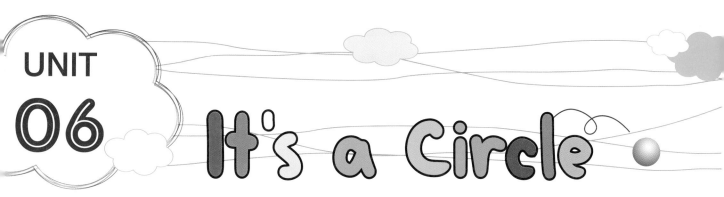

UNIT 06
It's a Circle

A Listen and chant.
Then circle the shapes you hear in the chant.

B Listen, circle, and match.

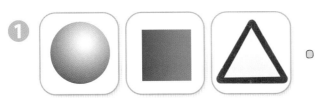

1. oval

2. pentagon

3. heart

4. triangle

C Listen, check, and circle the word.

1.
(star ❙ oval)

2.
(rectangle ❙ square)

3.
(heart ❙ square)

4.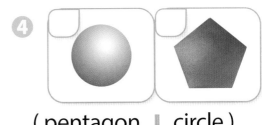
(pentagon ❙ circle)

D Listen, check, and match.

1   ◦   ◦ It's a pentagon.

2   ◦   ◦ It's an oval.

3   ◦   ◦ It's a rectangle.

4   ◦   ◦ It's a triangle.

E Listen, look, and circle "a" or "b".

① a / b   ② a / b   ③ a / b

④ a / b   ⑤ a / b   ⑥ a / b

SPEAK & PLAY

F Ask and answer with your partner. Follow the steps below.

Is it a/an _____?

Yes, it is./No, it isn't.
It's a/an _____.

circle   triangle   heart
oval   pentagon   square
star   rectangle

Step 1. 👆 Find a partner.

Step 2. 👆 Your partner asks you a question pointing a shape on the board, and then you answer it

Step 3. 👆 Find the Word Sticker for your answer.

Step 4. 👆 Attach the sticker below the shape.

WRITING

G Listen, circle, and write. **38**

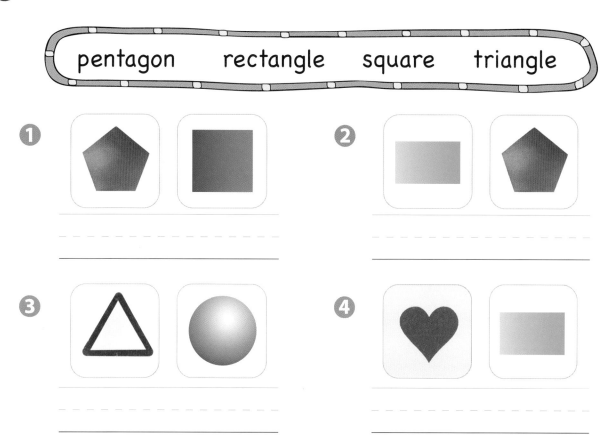

1

_____

2

_____

3

_____

4

_____

(word bank) pentagon   rectangle   square   triangle

H Read, look, and complete the sentences using "a" or "an".

1 Q Is it an oval?

A _____ , it is. It's _____ .

oval

2 Q Is it a circle?

A _____ , it isn't. It's _____ .

heart

I Listen and read the phonics story.

Flat face.
Black hair.
Blue blouse.
Flower skirt.
Doll on the blanket.

Is it a circle blanket?
No, it isn't.
Is it a square blanket?
Yes, it is.

J Listen and write the correct blend letters and a word.

> blouse   black   blue   flat   flower   blanket

1. _____ ➕ ack ➖ _____

2. _____ ➕ anket ➖ _____

3. _____ ➕ ouse ➖ _____

4. _____ ➕ ower ➖ _____

5. _____ ➕ ue ➖ _____

6. _____ ➕ at ➖ _____

UNIT 07

He's Short

CHANT LISTENING 40

A Listen and chant.
Then circle the adjectives you hear in the chant.

WORD LISTENING 🔞

B Listen, write the number, and match.

 ⭕  ⭕  ⭕  ⭕

⭕ **short** ⭕ **young** ⭕ **pretty** ⭕ **thin**

C Listen, look, and circle.

1    handsome   young   tall

2    old   short   fat

3    thin   fat   pretty

4   short   young   tall

SENTENCE LISTENING 🔵42

D Listen, check, and match.

1. ⚪ • He is fat.

2. ⚪ • He is short.

3. ⚪ • She is pretty.

4. ⚪ • She is young.

E Listen, look, and circle "a" or "b".

1. a / b

2. a / b

3. a / b

4. a / b

5. a / b

6. a / b

SPEAK & PLAY

F Ask and answer with your partner. Follow the steps below.

Is he/she _____?

Yes, he/she is. No, he/she isn't.
He/She is _____.

tall	short	old
young	pretty	handsome
fat	thin	

Step 1. Find a partner.

Step 2. Your partner asks you a question pointing an animal, and then you answer it.

Step 3. Find the Word Sticker for your answer.

Step 4. Attach the sticker below the animal.

WRITING

G Listen, circle, and write. **43**

pretty   tall   thin   young

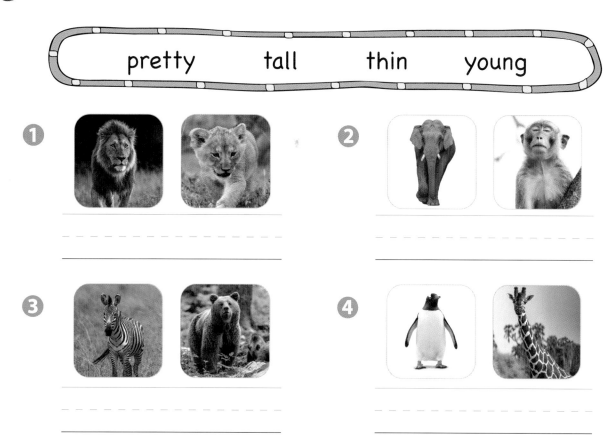

H Read, look, and complete the sentences.

1 Q Is she old?

    A _____ , she is. She is _____ .

old

2 Q Is he thin?

    A _____ , he isn't. He is _____ .

fat

PHONICS LISTENING 🔊44 〔S-Blends〕 **sm-, sn-**

I **Listen and read the phonics story.**

Snow! Snow!
It's snowing.

Smell some snacks.
Smoke some wood.
Snake sleeps.
Snowman smiles.
Is it small?
No, it isn't.

Snow! Snow!
I love snow.

J **Listen and circle the correct blend letters. Then write the right words.**

> smile   snake   small   smell   snowing   snowman

1. (sm- | sn-) _____

2. (sm- | sn-) _____

3. (sm- | sn-) _____

4. (sm- | sn-) _____

5. (sm- | sn-) _____

6. (sm- | sn-) _____

He Is Writing a Story

CHANT LISTENING 45

A Listen and chant.
Then circle the school activities you hear in the chant.

B Listen, circle, and match.

1    ∘

∘ drawing a picture

2   ∘

∘ writing a story

3   ∘

∘ using a computer

4  ∘

∘ reading a book

C Listen, check, and circle the word.

1

(speaking English ┃ reading a story)

2
(exercising ┃ singing a song)

3
(cutting paper ┃ drawing a picture)

4
(singing a song ┃ using a computer)

D Listen, check, and match.

1. ○ ○ She is drawing a picture.

2. ○ ○ He is writing a story.

3. ○ ○ He is exercising.

4. ○ ○ She is cutting paper.

E Listen, look, and circle "a" or "b".

1. a / b
2. a / b
3. a / b
4. a / b
5. a / b
6. a / b

SPEAK & PLAY

F Ask and answer with your partner. Follow the steps below.

What is he/she doing?

He/She is _____.

writing a story   drawing a picture
using a computer   cutting paper
singing a song   speaking English
reading a book   exercising

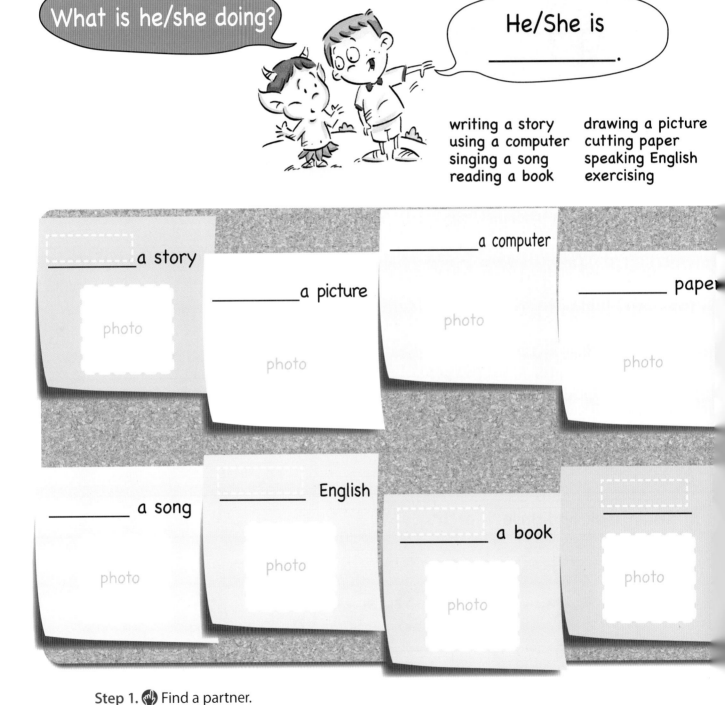

_____a story

photo

_____a picture

photo

_____a computer

photo

_____ paper

photo

_____ a song

photo

_____ English

photo

_____ a book

photo

_____

photo

Step 1. Find a partner.

Step 2. Your partner asks you a question, and then you answer it.

Step 3. Find the Activity Sticker for your answer.

Step 4. Attach the sticker on the right box, and then write the correct word.

WRITING

 Listen, circle, and write. 48

drawing a picture   using a computer   exercising   writing a story

①

_____

②

_____

③

_____

④

_____

H Read, look, and complete the sentences.

① **Q** What is he doing?

A He is _____ .

reading a book

② **Q** What is she doing?

A She is _____ .

speaking English

I Listen and read the phonics story.

Tent here.
Lamp there.
Jump high.
Hunt low.

What are they doing?
Camp, camp!
They're camping.

J Listen and write the correct blend letters and a word.

| tent | jump | hunt | lamp | camp | cent |

1. ca ➕ _____ ➖ _____
2. la ➕ _____ ➖ _____

3. te ➕ _____ ➖ _____
4. hu ➕ _____ ➖ _____

5. ju ➕ _____ ➖ _____
6. ce ➕ _____ ➖ _____

UNIT 09

I Like Math

CHANT LISTENING 50

A Listen and chant.
Then circle the school subjects you hear in the chant.

B Listen, write the number, and match.

(History) (Biology) (Science) (Geography)

C Listen, look, and circle.

①    Math   History   Art

②    Science   Art   Biology

③    Geography   Music   Math

④    Math   Science   English

SENTENCE LISTENING 🔵52

D Listen, check, and match.

1
○
○ Do you like Math?

2
○
○ Do you like English?

3
○
○ Do you like Science?

4
○
○ Do you like History?

E Listen, look, and circle "a" or "b".

1
a
b

2
a
b

3
a
b

4
a
b

5
a
b

6
a
b

SPEAK & PLAY

F Ask and answer with your partner. Follow the steps below.

Do you like _____?

Yes, I do./No, I don't.
I like _____.

Science   Math   English
History   Biology
Geography   Art   Music

Name Subjects		Shawn				
Science						
Math						
English		♡				
History						
Biology						
Geography						
Art						
Music						

Step 1. Find four partners, and then write their names.

Step 2. You ask them a question, and then they answer it.

Step 3. Attach the Heart Stickers for their answers.

WRITING

G Listen, circle, and write. **53**

Biology   Music   Science   Geography

①

_____

②

_____

③

_____

④

_____

H Read, look, and complete the sentences using "like".

① **Q** Do you like Science?

    A Yes, I do. I _____ .

Science

② **Q** Do you like Math?

    A No, I don't. I _____ .

Art

I **Listen and read the phonics story.**

I like frogs.
I like trees.
I like fruits.
I like trucks.
And I like Fridays.

Frank! Do you like friends?
Yes, I do.
I like my friends very much.

J **Listen and circle the correct blend letters. Then write the right words.**

fruit   truck   Friday   tree   frog   friend

1. (fr- | tr-) _____

2. (fr- | tr-) _____

3. (fr- | tr-) _____

4. (fr- | tr-) _____

5. (fr- | tr-) _____

6. (fr- | tr-) _____

UNIT 10

I Can Play the Piano

CHANT LISTENING 55

A Listen and chant.
Then circle the activities you hear in the chant.

B Listen, circle, and match.

1

2

3

4

- play the guitar
- play the violin
- play soccer
- play tennis

C Listen, check, and circle the word.

1

play baseball | play basketball

2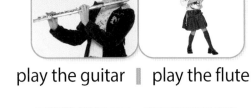

play the guitar | play the flute

3

play tennis | play the piano

4

play baseball | play the violin

SENTENCE LISTENING 🔊57

D Listen, check, and match.

1. ○   ○ I can play basketball.

2. ○   ○ I can play baseball.

3. ○   ○ I can play the guitar.

4. ○   ○ I can play the piano.

E Listen, look, and circle "a" or "b".

1. a / b
2. a / b
3. a / b
4. a / b
5. a / b
6. a / b

SPEAK & PLAY

F Ask and answer with your partner. Follow the steps below.

Can you play _____?

Yes, I can. I can play _____./
No, I can't. I can't play _____.

baseball   basketball   tennis
soccer   the flute   the piano
the violin   the guitar

the			

Step 1. Find a partner.

Step 2. Your partner asks you a question, and then you answer it using "the" or not.

Step 3. If you need "the", write "the" above the right picture.

Step 4. Find the Word Sticker for your answer.

Step 5. Attach the sticker below the right picture.

WRITING

 Listen, circle, and write. **58**

play baseball   play the guitar   play the piano   play tennis

1

_____

2

_____

3

_____

4

_____

H Read, look, and complete the sentences.

1 **Q** Can you play the flute?

   A _____ , I can. I can _____ .

play the flute

2 **Q** Can you play soccer?

   A _____ , I can't. I can't _____ .

play soccer

I Listen and read the phonics story.

Please! Please!
Can I play in the park?
Ride a plane.
Go down the slide.
Eat some plums.
Eat some slush.

Can I play in the park?
Yes, you can.

SLUSH
PARK

J Listen and write the correct blend letters and a word.

plane   please   slush   slide   play   plum

1. _____ ➕ ide ➖ _____   2. _____ ➕ um ➖ _____

3. _____ ➕ ane ➖ _____   4. _____ ➕ ease ➖ _____

5. _____ ➕ ush ➖ _____   6. _____ ➕ ay ➖ _____

Listen and write the letter "a", "b", or "c". 60

①

②

HISTORY

③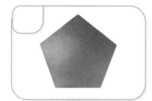

④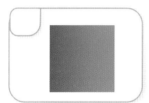

Hi

 Listen, unscramble the words, and match. 61

① rcilec → c_____ ○   ○

② xeercising → e_____ ○   ○

③ htors → s_____ ○   ○

④ thaM → M_____ ○   ○

C Listen and match. 🔢62

1. Do you like History? ○   ○ He is exercising.

2. Can you play the violin? ○   ○ No, it isn't. It's a circle.

3. Is it a square? ○   ○ Yes, he is. He is handsome.

4. Is he handsome? ○   ○ Yes, I can. I can play the violin.

5. What is he doing? ○   ○ No, I don't. I like Geography.

D Listen, find the picture, and write the number. 🔢63

E Listen, write the number, and match. 🔢64

☐	Can you speak English? ○	○	No, it isn't.
☐	What is she doing? ○	○	No, I don't.
☐	Is it a science? ○	○	Yes, I can.
☐	Do you like playing soccer? ○	○	She is playing the flute.

F Listen, look, and complete the sentences. 🔢65

can't   computers   do   using   No   old   play

❶

Q Is he young?

A _____, he isn't. He is _____.

❷

Q Do you like _____ _____?

A Yes, I _____.

❸

Q Can you _____ tennis?

A No, I _____. I can play the violin.

PHONICS REVIEW

G Listen to the words and circle them. 66

❶ flag ┃ plum ❷ blade ┃ sled ❸ smell ┃ snail ❹ jump ┃ dent

❺ try ┃ fry ❻ pump ┃ plane ❼ snap ┃ sleep ❽ pant ┃ plant

H Listen and check. 67

 ❶

❷

❸

❹

I Listen and circle the correct blend letters. Then write the right words. 68

1. (-mp ┃ -nt) _____

2. (sn- ┃ sm-) _____

3. (bl- ┃ br-) _____

4. (fr- ┃ tr-) _____

5. (-nt ┃ -mp) _____

6. (sn- ┃ sl-) _____

7. (fr- ┃ fl-) _____

8. (fl- ┃ pl-) _____

9. (bl- ┃ fr-) _____

10. (sl- ┃ sm-) _____

11. (-nt ┃ -mp) _____

12. (fr- ┃ tr-) _____

CHANT LIST

This is a cat. This is a cat.
This is a dog. This is a dog.
What is this? What is this?
This is a rabbit. This is a rabbit.
This is a goldfish. This is a goldfish.

What is that? What is that?
That is a turtle. That is a turtle.
That is an iguana. That is an iguana.
What is that? What is that?
That is a hamster. That is a hamster.
That is a parrot. That is a parrot.

What time is it?

Eleven. It's eleven o'clock.

Eleven ten. It's eleven ten.

What time is it?

Eleven twenty. It's eleven twenty.

Eleven thirty. It's eleven thirty.

What time is it?

Eleven forty. It's eleven forty.

Eleven fifty. It's eleven fifty.

What time is it?

Twelve. It's twelve o'clock.

Twelve fifteen. It's twelve fifteen.

How many bedrooms are there?

There are three bedrooms.

How many bathrooms are there?

There are two bathrooms.

How many livings rooms are there?

There is one living room.

How many dining rooms are there?

There is one dining room.

Bedroom, bathroom, living room, dining room.

How many kitchens are there?

There is one kitchen.

How many attics are there?

There is one attic.

How many basements are there?

There is one basement.

How many garages are there?

There is one garage.

Kitchen, attic, basement, garage.

Unit 4 I'm Going to the Park

Page 25

Where are you going? I'm going to the park.

Where? I'm going to the park.

Where are you going? I'm going to the museum.

Where? I'm going to the museum.

Where are you going? I'm going to the bank.

Where? I'm going to the bank.

Where are you going? I'm going to the hospital.

Where? I'm going to the hospital.

Where are you going? I'm going to the airport.

Where? I'm going to the airport.

Where are you going? I'm going to the post office.

Where? I'm going to the post office.

Where are you going? I'm going to the department store.

Where? I'm going to the department store.

Where are you going? I'm going to the library.

Where? I'm going to the library.

Unit 5 It's on the Bed

Page 31

Where is it? It's on the bed.

On, on. It's on the bed.

Where is it? It's under the desk.

Under, under. It's under the desk.

Where is it? It's in the closet.

In, in. It's in the closet.

Where is it? It's by the chair.

By, by. It's by the chair.

Where is it? It's on the bookshelf.
On, on. It's on the bookshelf.
Where is it? It's under the curtain.
Under, under. It's under the curtain.
Where is it? It's in the drawer.
In, in. It's in the drawer.
Where is it? It's by the lamp.
By, by. It's by the lamp.

Unit 6 It's a Circle 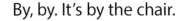 Page 41

Is it a triangle? Yes, it is. Yes, it is. It's a triangle.
Is it a circle? Yes, it is. Yes, it is. It's a circle.
Is it a square? Yes, it is. Yes, it is. It's a square.
Is it a rectangle? Yes, it is. Yes, it is. It's a rectangle.

Is it a star? No, it isn't. No, it isn't. It's an oval.
Is it an oval? No, it isn't. No, it isn't. It's a heart.
Is it a heart? No, it isn't. No, it isn't. It's a pentagon.
Is it a pentagon? No, it isn't. No, it isn't. It's a star.

Unit 7 He's Short Page 47

Tall, tall. Is he tall?
Yes, he is. He is tall.
Short, short. Is he short?
Yes, he is. He is short.
Young, young. Is she young?
Yes, she is. She is young.
Old, old. Is she old?
Yes, she is. She is old.
Tall and short. Young and old.

Fat, fat. Is he fat?

Yes, he is. He is fat.

Thin, thin. Is he thin?

Yes, he is. He is thin.

Pretty, pretty. Is she pretty?

Yes, she is. She is pretty.

Handsome, handsome. Is he handsome?

Yes, he is. He is handsome.

Fat and thin. Pretty and handsome.

Unit 8 He Is Writing a Story

Page 53

What is he doing? What is he doing?

He's writing a story. Writing a story.

He's reading a book. Reading a book.

What is she doing? What is she doing?

She's drawing a picture. Drawing a picture.

She's singing a song. Singing a song.

What is he doing? What is he doing?

He's using a computer. Using a computer.

He's exercising. Exercising.

What is she doing? What is she doing?

She's cutting paper. Cutting paper.

She's speaking English. Speaking English.

Unit 9 I Like Math

Page 59

Do you like Math?

Yes, I do. Yes, I do. I like Math.

Do you like English?

Yes, I do. Yes, I do. I like English.

Do you like History?

Yes, I do. Yes, I do. I like History.

Do you like Music?

Yes, I do. Yes, I do. I like Music.

Do You like Science?
No, I don't. No, I don't. I like Biology.
Do you like Biology?
No, I don't. No, I don't. I like Geography.
Do you like Geography?
No, I don't. No, I don't. I like Art.
Do you like Art?
No, I don't. No, I don't. I like Science.

Unit 10 I Can Play the Piano Page 65

Can you play the piano?
Yes, I can. I can play the piano.
Can you play the violin?
Yes, I can. I can play the violin.
Can you play the guitar?
Yes, I can. I can play the guitar.
Can you play the flute?
Yes, I can. I can play the flute.
Piano, violin, guitar, and flute.

Can you play soccer?
No, I can't. I can't play soccer.
Can you play baseball?
No, I can't. I can't play baseball.
Can you play basketball?
No, I can't. I can't play basketball.
Can you play tennis?
No, I can't. I can't play tennis.
Soccer, baseball, basketball, and tennis.

eleven o'clock   twelve o'clock   **twelve fifteen**

eleven fifty   eleven twenty   **twelve thirty**

twelve ten   eleven forty

one	one	one	one
two	two	two	two
three	three	three	three
four	four	four	four

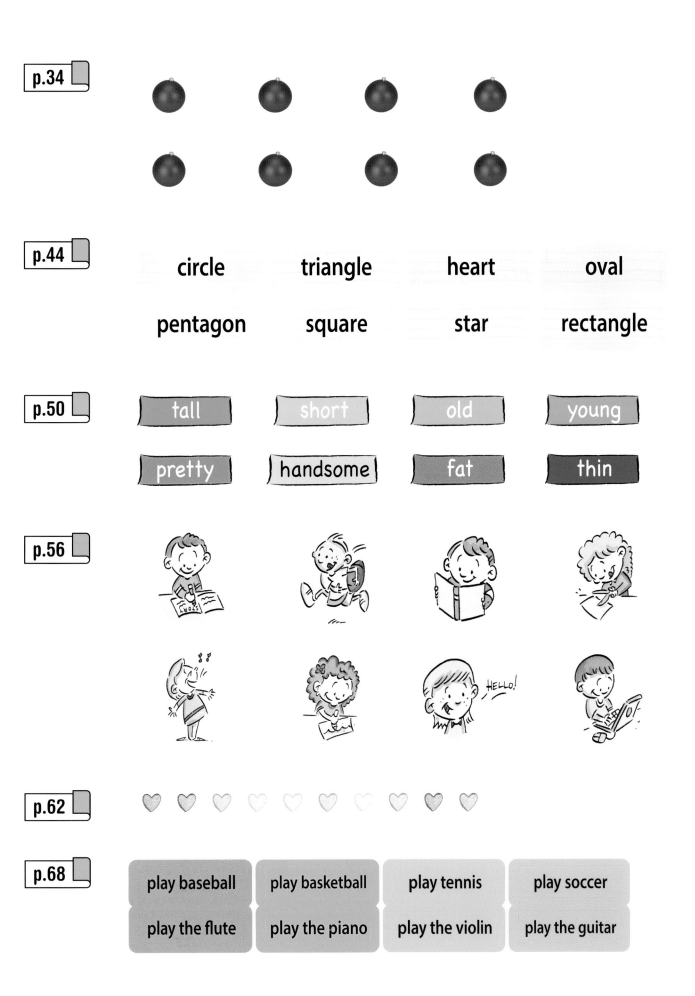

p.34

p.44

circle   triangle   heart   oval

pentagon   square   star   rectangle

p.50

tall   short   old   young

pretty   handsome   fat   thin

p.56

p.62

p.68

play baseball   play basketball   play tennis   play soccer

play the flute play the piano   play the violin play the guitar